THINKING SKILLS

Primary

Ready-to-go ideas and activities promoting
students' thinking skills across the curriculum.

Sharon Shapiro

Editor-in-Chief
Sharon Coan, M.S. Ed.

Art Director
CJae Froshay

Cover Artist
Lesley Plamer

Product Manager
Phil Garcia

Imaging
James Edward Grace

Publishers
Rachelle Cracchiolo, M.S. Ed.
Mary Dupuy Smith, M.S. Ed.

Blake Staff

Publisher
Sharon Dalgleish

Editor
Tricia Dearborn

Designed and illustrated by
Cliff Watt

Printed by
Printing Creations

INTRODUCTION

Today's students are the problem solvers of the future. However, in classrooms where teaching takes place at the level of factual knowledge only, the focus is on convergent thinking. Students learn to respond with conventionally correct answers rather than by exploring creative solutions.

All students can learn to think more critically and creatively. This book provides teachers with ideas and activities to help students develop these skills. The activities can be used to complement any classroom work in the various curriculum areas. They can be used in isolation, in sequence, or dipped into as teachers require.

In a future of guaranteed change, students will need to be adaptable. A grounding in creative thinking skills will enable them to pursue lifelong learning.

This edition published by

Teacher Created Materials, Inc.
6421 Industry Way
Westminster, CA 92683
www.teachercreated.com
©2001 Teacher Created Materials, Inc.
Made in U.S.A.
ISBN-0-7439-3623-X

with permission by
Blake Education
Locked Bag 2022
Glebe NSW 2037

CONTENTS

Task cards which draw together and consolidate skills taught in the Quick Starts and work sheets, containing clear step-by-step instructions for students

HOW TO USE THIS BOOK

TEACHERS' FILE

This section shows teachers how to make make the most of this book. It explains the reasons for strategies and suggestions for their use. It contains ideas for classroom organization as well as background notes, technology tips, assessment ideas, and suggestions for parent involvement.

QUICK STARTS

This section is written for teachers and includes activities, games, and ideas which will help teachers promote children's thinking skills. These activities can be used at any time, with little or no preparation, in any order, and incorporated across various curriculum areas to complement the regular classroom curriculum.

TAKE YOUR OWN TIME

This section contains 29 reproducible pages, covering topic areas such as Fluency, Flexibility, Categorizing, Questioning, Imaginative Visualization, Creative and Critical Thinking, and Originality. The pages can be used in any sequence and may also be modified and adapted to suit individual students or classes.

STEP BY STEP

This section contains task cards written for students. These can be used in activity centers for contract work at any time and in any sequence. Group and individual activities are included. They are aimed at older students in the primary grades, because of the reading required and the necessity for students to be able to follow instructions and complete the task independently.

TEACHERS' FILE

BACKGROUND NOTES

What is a thinking skill?

In addition to helping us think clearly, thinking skills help us critically and creatively collect information to effectively solve problems. As a result of learning thinking skills, students will also become more aware of decision-making processes.

Improved thinking encourages students to look at a variety of ideas, search to greater depth, practice more critical decision-making, challenge accepted ideas, approach tasks in decisive ways, and search for misunderstandings, while keeping the aims of the task clearly in mind.

The end results will be decisions that are more reliable, deeper understanding of concepts, contributions that are more creative, content that is examined more critically, and products that are more carefully crafted.

Why do students need to develop thinking skills?

Students need to develop the abilities to judge, analyze, and think critically in order to function in a democratic and technological society. A school as a whole should value the development of thinking skills and provide opportunities for these processes to be modeled and developed. Thinking skills can be taught, and all students can improve their thinking abilities. Creativity is present in all children regardless of age, race, socioeconomic status, and different learning modes.

The basic skills are generally considered to be reading, writing, and mathematics. These processes involve computation, recall of facts, and the basic mechanics of writing. Teachers should encourage mastery of basic skills as quickly as possible. Then avoid simply giving students more of the same work, as this merely creates boredom and frustration and reduces the children's opportunities to reach complex levels of understanding.

Unfortunately, research shows that too many teachers believe that if students calculate the correct answers to problems, they have learned thinking skills. Frequently, students are faced with tasks that expect them to demonstrate their ability to use higher-level thinking without having had the opportunities to develop their abilities with these thinking processes. The cognitive operations that make up thinking need to be explored, explained, taught, and practiced many times before they are mastered.

Some basic tips

Allow students to be nonconforming and encourage them to complete tasks in their own way. Encourage them to take risks, challenge ideas, and reflect on tasks. If a child learns hundreds of facts but hasn't developed the ability to explore possibilities, much of the knowledge they gain will be wasted.

Thinking domains

It is desirable to develop different thinking domains, as they have different aims and develop different skills:

- *Critical thinking* examines, clarifies, and evaluates an idea, belief, or action's reasonableness. Students need to infer, generalize, take a point of view, hypothesize, and find temporary solutions.
- Brainstorming, linking ideas, using analogies, creating original ideas, organizing information, and looking at a problem from different perspectives will lead to alternative solutions useful in *decision making* and *problem solving*.
- The *collection*, *retention*, *recall*, and *use* of information when needed is another vital skill.
- *Creative thinking* aims for original ideas.

Thinking Processes

Eight processes, divisible into cognitive and affective abilities, have been identified as being important in fostering thinking skills:

Cognitive abilities
- *Fluency* takes place when as many ideas as possible are thought of by students.
- *Flexibility* happens when students look at problems from different perspectives and think of ways to combine unusual ideas into something new and different. At times objects may have to be grouped according to different criteria.
- *Originality* involves producing unusual or unique ideas.
- *Elaboration* involves adding or further developing ideas.

Affective (feeling) abilities
- *Curiosity* involves working out an idea by instinctively following a pathway.
- *Complexity* involves thinking of more complex ways of approaching a task. This may involve searching for links, looking for missing sections, or restructuring ideas.
- *Risk-taking* is seen in students who guess and defend their ideas without fear that others will make fun of their thoughts.
- *Imaginative* students can picture and instinctively create what has never occurred, and imagine themselves in other times and places.

ASSESSMENT

Allow time for completion of activities and create opportunities for responses to be shared in a group. One way students learn is by mirroring the behavior and responses of others. As general rules:
- Do not grade activities, but display them.
- Do not criticize students' responses or drawings.
- Find something to value whenever possible.

There needs to be continuity in the way students are assessed, so that information is cumulative and accurate. A progressive file for each child should include information about their strengths, weaknesses, and any special achievements or creative results they have achieved.

Note carefully any changes or unusual results or progress, especially in highly creative areas such as story writing, art, special projects, research, inventions, or music. Encourage students to examine and assess their own abilities and goals to obtain insight into themselves and the way they tackle a problem.

For a reproducible sheet of fun awards for proficiency in thinking skills, see page 44.

CLASSROOM ORGANIZATION

The classroom environment

The learning environment should allow for creative expression nurtured by questions, tasks, exploration, and play. Create flexible working and seating spaces so that students have greater freedom to move around to different areas of the classroom, depending on tasks they are completing. Develop areas for independent work, small-group work, and areas where the whole class can meet. Bring in carpet squares or mats, bean bags, and pillows so students can work comfortably while sitting on the floor or working in groups.

Vary the shape of areas and the color of different sections of the classroom to vary the mood and create interest. By including shapes such as hexagons, pentagons, spheres, and domes, scope is created to challenge students with numerous environmental problems. Colors can be used to set the mood for the type of work students will be doing in a vicinity. Red will stimulate thought, orange will energize the children, while yellow will vitalize and accelerate mental activities. Green and blue soothe and calm over-excited students and are ideal to incorporate in a quiet reading area.

Organize materials systematically so students have easy access to them. Use open shelving, boxes, cartons, wine cask boxes, and ice-cream buckets to store activities and resources.

Learning centers

Learning centers should have a wealth of activities that challenge every child and encourage them to learn in different ways. Establish a routine for the process of selecting cards so that students know how many can work at each station at a time. Explain which activities are compulsory and where there is a choice, and formulate procedures for students to follow when they have incomplete cards. For young children, activities should incorporate a number of picture symbols and words, and tape recorders can be used to record some of the more detailed responses.

Create an interest center that has actual machines such as egg beaters, toy machines, and cameras, and set up a stimulus activity center which includes dress-up clothes, books, and unusual toys.

Aim for diversity and balance

Ensure that there is variety in the way students are working. Encourage them to work independently at times, in small groups, with older students, or as peer tutors.

Strive for a balance between structured and unstructured tasks and convergent and divergent tasks. Encourage students to use techniques that change from hands-on, to visual, oral, or written, so a variety of learning styles are used. At different times and for different tasks, it is best to discuss, dramatize, or work from contracts or at learning centers. This variety will help with active involvement, thinking skills, motivation, and longer periods of concentration.

TECHNOLOGY TIPS

Computer games can be used to motivate students and encourage task commitment. When software is carefully selected, it can be used to develop higher-order thinking skills. Simulation or strategy software is motivational and open-ended, involving players in critical thinking, risk-taking, and real-life problem solving.

Computing skills can be integrated into many aspects of the learning experience. Computer technology is useful for programming and problem solving. LOGO language has been written with children in mind. Children can type in instructions to create individual designs and drawings. Spread sheets and data bases develop higher-order skills and lateral thinking. They will also develop a spatial orientation. A program called *Thinkin' Things*, containing age appropriate activities, is available from Edmark.

Technology in the form of board games can be used to encourage and develop thinking skills. Students learn rules and apply different strategies in games such as Chess, Abalone, and Scrabble.

PARENT INVOLVEMENT

Let parents know that there are many opportunities to develop students' thinking skills when they are playing at home. A simple exercise such as packing the groceries away in a cupboard, refrigerator, or freezer after a shopping trip involves students in sorting and grouping the items that go in the freezer and those that should be kept in the refrigerator. It is a wonderful opportunity to discuss which items are the same and which are different.

This activity can be further developed if it is followed with a "What if?" question. For example, ask children, "What would happen if we put the ice cream in the cupboard instead of in the freezer?" "What would happen to the honey if it was put in the freezer instead of the cupboard?"

Parents can ask students to help sort items such as pencils, socks, spoons, and forks so students will begin to categorize and classify.

Students can also be given opportunities to work creatively at home, making objects using empty boxes, milk cartons, cardboard rolls, styrofoam cups, paper plates, and left-over items.

There are many questions that parents can ask of themselves: Do our children have opportunities to work on problems where creative thinking is valued? Are they given opportunities at home to write story endings differently and apply history's lessons to today's problems? Are they involved in planning family outings that will satisfy the needs of all members? Are they allowed to participate in family projects such as redesigning rooms? Most importantly, are they encouraged to be part of an environment where it is acceptable to make mistakes, and where the focus is on learning from them?

QUICK STARTS

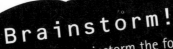

Brainstorm!

Have students in groups brainstorm the following topics:
Name all the things that move.
What things are found underground?
List everything that is pink.
Emphasize that there are no right or wrong answers and the aim is quantity not quality. Have groups share their answers with the class so that students can learn from those who think more divergently.

How could you...?

Have students in groups, or as a class, list:

• all the different ways they could travel to school tomorrow.
• how they could make people laugh.
• other ways to use a magazine besides reading it.
• the different uses for a spoonful of peanut butter.

Car Parts

Using an old but large toy car, ask students to imagine it is a full-sized car, and explain that the car no longer works but is being broken into parts. What uses can they think of for the different parts of the car? For example, a front bench seat could become a sofa, tires could be used as swings, a headlight could become a bedlamp...

It won't happen!

Ask students to name:
• 10 things they can't hear
• 5 people they will never meet
• 7 things that can't be photographed

What's the connection?

Ask students to tell you the connection between two line drawings, for example, a picture of rain and a square. In this instance, the square might be a farmer's field that the rain falls on. There is no wrong answer if a link can be explained.

Clever Categories

Ask students to divide these words into groups, according to categories they decide on:
girl   butter   castle   apple   forest   cake   chair   unicorn   cat   fairy   train   frog   sock   egg   tree   waterfall   bicycle   fire engine

(The words can be written onto a sheet of paper that is photocopied and cut up so each group has a set. This allows students to physically move the words between categories and see the effect.)

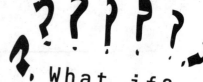

What if?

Encourage students to explore alternatives:

- What if students all grew three feet taller in the night?
- What if it rained milk?
- What if people were born old and got younger?

Crazy Combinations

Ask students to brainstorm a list of different fruit. Follow this with a list of different animals. Have students work in pairs and ask them to draw an *anifruit* by combining features of one of the animals and one of the fruits. Have them give their *anifruit* a name, for example, a combination of an apricot and a cat could be an *apricat*, or they can just invent a name that feels appropriate.

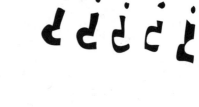

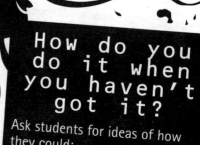

How do you do it when you haven't got it?

Ask students for ideas of how they could:

- brush their hair without a hairbrush or comb.
- write a story without pencil or paper.
- get dressed without using clothes.

Predicting the Future

Ask students:

- what they think children will wear to school in 100 years' time
- what they think they will be doing, and where they will be, in twenty years
- how they will travel to school in the future

Imagine that!

- Have students cut pictures out of magazines and join different heads, bodies, and other items to invent strange people and things.
- Ask students to imagine what is inside a house they see in a picture.

The Inventors

Have students invent:

- a new way to brush their hair
- a machine for cleaning a budgie's cage
- a device that wakes them up in the morning and feeds them breakfast

Fix it!

Using an item children are familiar with, for example, a cup or a pencil, ask them to tell you what are its disadvantages. For example, the cup can spill stuff on your face if you tip it up quickly. Have students suggest ideas for fixing the problem, for example, a guard that extends from the rim of the cup but leaves room for your mouth. Encourage silly and unusual ideas.

Recycle

Ask students what they could do with:

- felt-tip pens that don't write anymore
- a trampoline that has lost its bounce
- cereal that has gone stale

It doesn't matter how silly the ideas are. Encourage students to think of as many as they can.

What is the same?

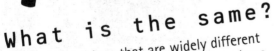

Think of two things that are widely different and ask students what these two things have in common; for example, for a train and an apple, both can be red; both can be shiny; it's healthy for your body to eat apples and healthy for the environment to catch a train rather than drive a car.

The Evolving Classroom

Have students as a class, brainstorm ways that the classroom could be made a more comfortable, exciting, and interesting place. Ask students in groups to choose one of the possible changes and think of what would need to be done to make the change. With the students, implement any realistic ideas that come out of this activity.

BAR

B stands for bigger/smaller.

A stands for add on.

R stands for replace/rearrange/change.

For example, draw a shoe. Then use BAR.

What could be made Bigger or smaller? The sole of the shoe could be a platform three feet high so you could see over people's heads in a crowd.

What could be Added? Wings or a motor would speed you along.

What could be Replaced? Laces could become Velcro strips so it is easier to get your shoes off.

Try BAR with a bed or a pencil, giving reasons for each change. Encourage silly and innovative ideas.

How many ways can you ...?

Have students in groups find as many ways as they can think of to:

- get from their bedrooms to their kitchens.
- blow up a balloon.
- put their clothes on.

Reflecting on the Day

At the end of each day, ask children what they learned during the day, what new things they found out, what they did well, and what they could learn to do better. Reinforce the positive aspects of the day. Help children think of something to tell their parents about or ways to use their new thinking skills at home.

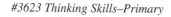

Alphabet Animals

Find names of animals for each letter of the alphabet. Write as many as you can think of for each letter. For D you could have dog, duck, dinosaur, deer . . .

A _____   N _____

B _____   O _____

C _____   P _____

D _____   Q _____

E _____   R _____

F _____   S _____

G _____   T _____

H _____   U _____

I _____   V _____

J _____   W _____

K _____   X _____

L _____   Y _____

M _____   Z _____

Thinking skill: Fluency

What Could It Be?

Work in a group to think of all the answers that you can to the questions. See if other students' answers give you more ideas. One student could write a list or tape the responses.

How many things are smaller than your hand?
List them.

_____

_____

_____

_____

_____

What can be hidden under your shoe?

_____

_____

_____

_____

What can you balance on your hand?

_____

_____

_____

Thinking skill: Fluency

What Did You See Today?

What did you see when you first woke up today? when you walked through the house? on your way to school? List everything you have seen today.

_____

_____

_____

_____

_____

_____

_____

_____

_____

_____

_____

_____

_____

Thinking skill: Fluency

How Can You Use It?

Work in a small group. Take a paper clip each and hold it, feel it, open it, bend it, reshape it.

How many different uses can you think of for a paper clip?

hairclip

letter of the alphabet

Thinking skill: Fluency

Do You Want a Ride?

How many different things can you ride?

_____

_____

_____

_____

_____

_____

_____

List all the things that you can push.

_____

_____

_____

_____

_____

Thinking skill: Fluency

Playing Games

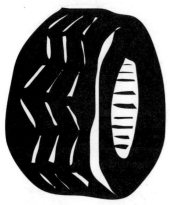

Imagine an old tire. What does it look like? How heavy is it? What does it feel like? What does it smell like?

How many games, using an old car tire, can you make up?

_____

_____

_____

_____

If the tire was chopped into pieces, how could you use the different bits? Note that some bits of the tire are rough, some are smooth, and some have letters on them.

_____

_____

_____

_____

_____

Thinking skill: Fluency

Make a Picture

Choose a shape and change it into:

a car	a house	an imaginary friend	a dog

Thinking skill: Flexibility

What Are These? →

1. If they are eyes, what is ? _____

2. If they are heads, what are ? _____

3. If they are balls, what is ? _____

4. If they are hoops, what is ? _____

5. If they are earrings, what is ? _____

6. If they are round windows, what is ? _____

7. If they are holes in the road, what is ? _____

8. If they are oranges, what is ? _____

Thinking skill: Flexibility

A Piece of String

Get a 12 inch (30 cm) piece of string from your teacher. Write down all the things you could do with your piece of string.

_____

_____

_____

_____

_____

_____

_____

_____

_____

_____

Thinking skill: Flexibility

The Old Fire Engine

This fire engine is too old to be used as a fire engine anymore. It's going to be pulled to pieces. What could all the pieces be used for?

wheels _____

ladder _____

headlights _____

seats _____

steering wheel _____

windshield _____

hose _____

other pieces _____

Thinking skill: Flexibility

What Is the Same?
What Is Different?

Use the acronym SCUMPS to compare the objects.
List everything that is the same or different.

S = Size _____

_____

C = Color _____

_____

U = Use _____

_____

M = Materials _____

_____

P = Parts _____

_____

S = Shape _____

_____

Thinking skill: Flexibility

The Pink Shirt

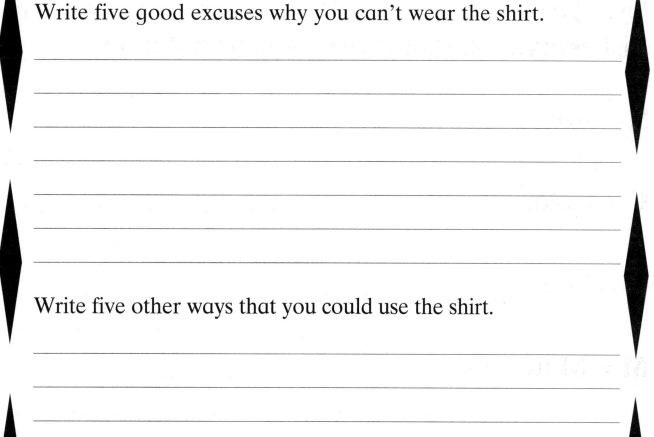

For your birthday your grandmother has given you a pink shirt that you hate. You don't want to hurt her feelings, but you don't want to wear it.

Write five good excuses why you can't wear the shirt.

_____

_____

_____

_____

_____

_____

_____

Write five other ways that you could use the shirt.

_____

_____

_____

_____

_____

_____

Thinking skill: Flexibility

What Can It Be Used For?

Write at least 10 uses for a tennis ball.
They can be as silly as you like.

Thinking skill: Flexibility

28

What a Face!

Divide these faces into groups. Explain your reasons for the groups.

_____

_____

_____

_____

_____

_____

_____

_____

_____

_____

_____

_____

Thinking skill: Categorizing

You Ask the Questions

The answer is "a rose." Write at least 3 questions.

_____

_____

_____

_____

_____

The answer is "In the middle of the night."
Write at least 3 questions.

_____

_____

_____

_____

_____

Thinking skill: Questioning

What Can It Be?

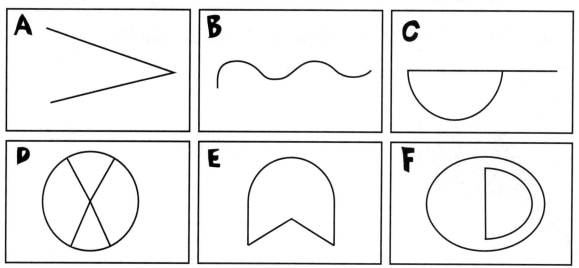

Look at the pictures and write what you think they could be. You can look at them upside down or any way.

It's something to do with school. What is it?	It's something to do with the holidays. What is it?
A _____	A _____
B _____	B _____
C _____	C _____
D _____	D _____
E _____	E _____
F _____	F _____

Thinking skill: Imaginative visualization

The *Trancapar*

Draw a *trancapar*. (There is no such thing as a *trancapar*, so it can be anything you like.)

Tell the story of what happened to the trancapar last Tuesday.

_____

_____

_____

_____

_____

Thinking skill: Imaginative visualization

What Are These Splotches?

Example:
This is a baby bird with its beak open. It is crying for food.

Write in the space what each splotch could be.

Thinking skill: Imaginative visualization

Create a Picture

Sample:
See what a
triangle
can be.

Below is a square. Add lines and shapes
to make a picture.

Thinking skill: Imaginative visualization

Jack and the Beanstalk

Imagine that Jack is climbing up the beanstalk. Draw four different pictures of what he might have seen as he got higher and higher.

Thinking skill: Imaginative visualization

Is It a Ghost?

Write down all the things that this cloud looks like.

_____

_____

_____

_____

_____

_____

_____

_____

_____

_____

Thinking skill: Imaginative visualization

Change the Chair

Redesign the chair by using the BAR system.

B = make it bigger or smaller

A = add something

R = remove something and replace it with something else

B

Reasons _____

_____

A

Reasons _____

_____

R

Reasons _____

_____

Thinking skill: Creative thinking

Help the Kangaroo

A kangaroo hurt its leg while hopping. It can't move and needs to be taken to a vet. Draw four different ways of moving the kangaroo so that it can be taken to the vet. Label each drawing.

Thinking skill: Creative thinking

38

Toothpick Tricks

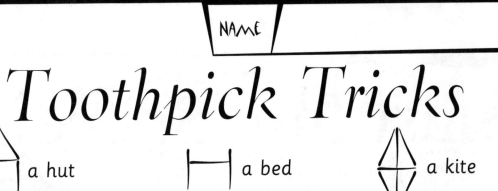

a hut   a bed   a kite

Try making different pictures, using no more than 8 toothpicks for each. (No breaking the toothpicks!) Use glue to stick your favorite picture to the page.

Some pictures to try: a fan, an insect, a flag, a dog, a spaceship, a fish, a windmill, a tent

Thinking skill: Creative thinking

Blast Into Space

Make something that can be used in space.

You'll need:

a box
2 cardboard tubes
a cup
glue stick or sticky tape
a pair of scissors
other objects available in your classroom

Draw your design for the thing you are going to make in the box below. Then build it.

Thinking skill: Creative thinking

What Is THAT?

Make up a new and strange animal and draw it here.

What is it called?

Where does it live?

What does it eat?

Thinking skill: Originality

Join the Pictures

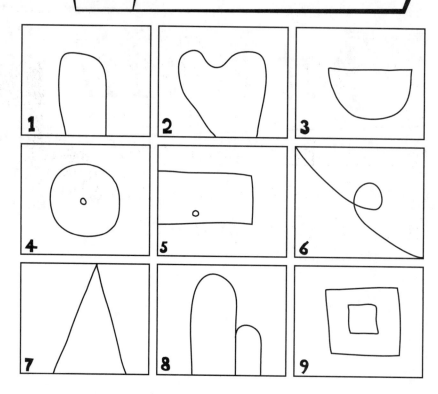

1. If picture 1 is a finger, what is 4? _____

2. If picture 7 is a mountain, what is 6? _____

3. If picture 2 is a tooth, what is 3? _____

4. If picture 8 is a kennel, what is 9? _____

5. If picture 4 is a hat (you are looking down on it), what is 5?

_____

6. If picture 8 is an igloo, what is 4? _____

7. If picture 8 shows two rocks, what is 1? _____

8. If picture 5 is a door (turn the page sideways), what do you see

   when you open the door and find picture 9? _____

Thinking skill: Originality

42

What a Tale!

Make up a story about the toaster and the cat. You can add other characters and objects as you write.

_____

_____

_____

_____

_____

_____

_____

_____

_____

_____

Thinking skill: Connecting unrelated objects

Thinking Skills Awards

Awarded to
_____

Terrific thinking!

Signed _____

Date _____

Awarded to
_____

Good idea!

Signed _____

Date _____

Awarded to
_____

Great imagination!

Signed _____

Date _____

Awarded to
_____

Clever question!

Signed _____

Date _____

STEP BY STEP

Skill: Creative thinking

Build a Tower

What you need:

- 30 straws
- masking tape
- 3 foam cups
- paper clips

What to do:

1. Talk with one or two friends about how you will build a tower using the materials listed.

2. Build your tower.

3. Organize a competition with other students doing this activity. You could give awards to (a) the tallest tower (b) the steadiest tower (c) the silliest tower.

Tip: you can tape the straws together or push one end into the other.

Skills: Imaginative visualization and flexibility

Blind Drawing

What you need:

- a blindfold
- a large piece of paper
- a pencil

What to do:

1. Put your paper and pencil in front of you on the desk. Decide what you are going to draw; then blindfold your eyes. Make sure you can't see at all.

2. When you have finished your drawing, take the blindfold off and look at it. DON'T ERASE ANY LINES!

3. Finish the picture by adding extra lines, color, or decorations.

4. Here are some things you could try drawing: a person's face with two eyes, a nose, and mouth; a tree, two flowers and the sun; an animal sitting on some grass; the moon, stars, and a rocket ship. Think of your own as well!

 **TASK CARD 3**

Create an Animal

What you need:
- a paper plate
- a milk carton
- scissors
- glue

What to do:

1. Decide on the animal you want to make.
2. Find a picture in a book or draw what it will look like.
3. Decide which way the carton will stand. Does the animal have a long or short body? Is it tall? How many legs and eyes does it have? Does it have a tail?
4. Cut the paper plate into the pieces you need. Think of the shape and size of the parts you are making. Are they rough or smooth? Choose the parts of the plate that you need. Do you need to fold as well as cut it?
5. Glue your animal together. When it has dried, paint the body and decorate it.

 **TASK CARD 4**

Question Time

What to do:

1. Choose one person to sit in front (the *chooser*) and one person to keep count of how many questions have been asked (the *counter*). The rest of the group sits in front of the caller.

2. The *chooser* chooses an animal, thing, or famous person but must not tell anyone else what or who it is.

3. The rest of the group asks questions to try to guess what or who it is. The questions must have the answer "yes" or "no." (If the *chooser* doesn't know, it doesn't count as a question.) The group gets 15 questions.

4. If the group can't guess, the *chooser* says what it was and has another turn. If someone guesses the right answer, the *chooser* sits down and the person with the correct answer becomes the new *chooser*. Change the *counter* for each game.

The Infobot, Part 1

What you need:

- pencil
- paper
- cardboard boxes
- glue
- magazines
- nails
- knobs
- springs
- paper cups
- string
- other scrap materials

What to do:

1. Think about what you want your robot to look like. What body parts might it have? How could you make them using the materials that you have?

2. Draw a picture (a design) of what you want your robot to look like.

3. Build your robot's body and add anything else you wish. You might like to make a sign that says, "Ask the Infobot!"

Bees live in a beehive.

The Infobot, Part 2

What you need:

- your robot
- a tape recorder
- a blank tape

What to do:

1. Research a topic that you are interested in, for example, baseball, the solar system, or dinosaurs. Collect all the interesting information that you can. Keep notes on what you find out.

2. Select what information you want to pass on, and put it in an order you think will help others understand it.

3. Record the information clearly onto the blank tape. (Ask your teacher to help you.)

4. Label the tape and place the recorder behind the Infobot. Other students can sit in front of Infobot and listen to the tape.